Social Programs
Democrats
Would Vote For

If they had to pay for them with their own money

A Comprehensive Analysis

This book belongs to:

_____

This Page Intentionally Left Blank

This Page Intentionally Left Blank

This Page Intentionally Left Blank

This Page Intentionally Left Blank

This Page Intentionally Left Blank

This Page Intentionally Left Blank

This Page Intentionally Left Blank

This Page Intentionally Left Blank

This Page Intentionally Left Blank

This Page Intentionally Left Blank

This Page Intentionally Left Blank

This Page Intentionally Left Blank

This Page Intentionally Left Blank

This Page Intentionally Left Blank

This Page Intentionally Left Blank

33

This Page Intentionally Left Blank

This Page Intentionally Left Blank

This Page Intentionally Left Blank

This Page Intentionally Left Blank

This Page Intentionally Left Blank

This Page Intentionally Left Blank

This Page Intentionally Left Blank

This Page Intentionally Left Blank

This Page Intentionally Left Blank

This Page Intentionally Left Blank

This Page Intentionally Left Blank

This Page Intentionally Left Blank

This Page Intentionally Left Blank

This Page Intentionally Left Blank

This Page Intentionally Left Blank

This Page Intentionally Left Blank

This Page Intentionally Left Blank

This Page Intentionally Left Blank

This Page Intentionally Left Blank

This Page Intentionally Left Blank

This Page Intentionally Left Blank

This Page Intentionally Left Blank

This Page Intentionally Left Blank

This Page Intentionally Left Blank

This Page Intentionally Left Blank

This Page Intentionally Left Blank

This Page Intentionally Left Blank

This Page Intentionally Left Blank

This Page Intentionally Left Blank

This Page Intentionally Left Blank

This Page Intentionally Left Blank

This Page Intentionally Left Blank

This Page Intentionally Left Blank

This Page Intentionally Left Blank

This Page Intentionally Left Blank

This Page Intentionally Left Blank

This Page Intentionally Left Blank

This Page Intentionally Left Blank

This Page Intentionally Left Blank

This Page Intentionally Left Blank

This Page Intentionally Left Blank

This Page Intentionally Left Blank

This Page Intentionally Left Blank

This Page Intentionally Left Blank

This Page Intentionally Left Blank

Made in the USA
Las Vegas, NV
25 September 2021